D1607434

Great White
Sharks

THIS EDITION
Editorial Management by Oriel Square
Produced for DK by WonderLab Group LLC
Jennifer Emmett, Erica Green, Kate Hale, *Founders*

Editors Grace Hill Smith, Libby Romero, Maya Myers, Michaela Weglinski;
Photography Editors Kelley Miller, Annette Kiesow, Nicole DiMella; **Managing Editor** Rachel Houghton;
Designers Project Design Company; **Researcher** Michelle Harris; **Copy Editor** Lori Merritt;
Indexer Connie Binder; **Proofreader** Larry Shea; **Reading Specialist** Dr. Jennifer Albro;
Curriculum Specialist Elaine Larson

Published in the United States by DK Publishing
1745 Broadway, 20th Floor, New York, NY 10019

Copyright © 2023 Dorling Kindersley Limited
DK, a Division of Penguin Random House LLC
23 24 25 26 10 9 8 7 6 5 4 3 2 1
001-334130-Sept/2023

A catalog record for this book
is available from the Library of Congress.
HC ISBN: 978-0-7440-7588-5
PB ISBN: 978-0-7440-7589-2

DK books are available at special discounts when purchased in bulk for sales promotions, premiums,
fundraising, or educational use. For details, contact: DK Publishing Special Markets,
1745 Broadway, 20th Floor, New York, NY 10019
SpecialSales@dk.com

Printed and bound in China

The publisher would like to thank the following for their kind permission to reproduce their images:
a=above; c=center; b=below; l=left; r=right; t=top; b/g=background

Alamy Stock Photo: David Fleetham 22-23, Nature Picture Library 24-25, Nature Picture Library / Chris & Monique Fallows 30-31,
Harry Stone 14, WaterFrame_fba 27cra; **BluePlanetArchive.com:** C & M Fallows 23br, James D. Watt 20-21, Doc White 15tr;
Dreamstime.com: Alcaproac 19, Hakoar 27tl, Irko Van Der Heide 24tr, Hotshotsworldwide 26clb, Isselee 26br, Izanbar 10-11,
Nerthuz 1b, Sergiy1975 8bl, Slowmotiongli 3cb, Sombra12 27tr, Sergey Uryadnikov 12-13, 13tl, 16-17, Olga Usatova 27clb,
Whitepointer 18t; **Getty Images:** Corbis Documentary / Clouds Hill Imaging Ltd. 11ca, Image Source / Rodrigo Friscione 28-29,
The Image Bank / Stephen Frink 27br; **Getty Images / iStock:** EMPPhotography 8-9, Michel Viard 28bl, vladoskan 7br;
Science Photo Library: Chris & Monique Fallows / Nature Picture Library 7, SCUBAZOO 4-5;
Shutterstock.com: Dirk van der Heide 26cr, Alessandro De Maddalena 12cr, wildestanimal 32b

Cover images: *Front:* **Shutterstock.com:** Martin Prochazkacz; *Back:* **Dreamstime.com:** Baksiabat clb, Lidiia Lykova cra

All other images © Dorling Kindersley
For more information see: www.dkimages.com

For the curious
www.dk.com

Great White Sharks

Ruth A. Musgrave

Contents

Fierce Fish

A mouthful of sharp, saw-like teeth. Big jaws, opened wide. A pointy fin that sticks up out of the water.

Such features make the great white shark one of the most feared animals on Earth. It is true that great whites are fierce hunters. But they do not hunt people. These big fish prefer to keep their distance from us.

Let's get up close and find out what makes great whites such powerful ocean predators.

Also Known As ...

Great whites are also called white pointers.

Keeping Cool

Great whites live throughout the world in cooler ocean waters.

Baby Great Whites

Great whites already know how to swim, hunt, and hide from predators when they are born.

Not So Little

Newborn great white pups can be as long as a bicycle.

Great white shark mothers give birth near shore. The shallow water is a safer place for little sharks to grow up. Larger predators hunt in the deep water. They don't usually hunt close to shore.

Pups are born with a mouthful of sharp teeth.

Great Whites, Inside and Out

Great white sharks are big. A large great white is longer than a car. It weighs as much as a car, too.

Great whites, like all sharks, do not have bones. Their skeleton is made of the same material as your ears. It is light and bends easily. This helps the shark make quick turns as it swims.

Tough scales cover and protect a shark's skin. Its skin feels like sandpaper.

A great white's body is shaped like a football. That helps it move fast through the water.

This shark's colors help it hide. Its gray back blends in with the dark sea below. Its white belly blends in with the light from the water's surface.

Sharks have many fins. Their front fins help them turn and stop. Their other fins help them keep their balance when they swim fast or make sharp turns.

Fin Form

Sharks cannot fold their fins.

Stay Away

Great whites sometimes use their tail to keep other sharks away from their food.

Sharks move their tail side to side to swim. Strong muscles give the tail its power. Its shape helps the shark swim fast.

fin

No Thank You

Sharks have taste buds inside their mouth and throat. These help sharks know if something is tasty or not. Sharks will sometimes take a test bite and then spit out what they don't like.

A great white shark's big teeth are shaped like triangles. Each tooth has bumpy edges.

All sharks have many rows of teeth. They lose teeth when they eat. When one tooth falls out, a tooth from the row behind moves up into its place.

A great white uses its teeth to grab prey. The sharp teeth cut the food into pieces. Then the shark swallows the chunks whole.

Sensational Senses

Great whites use all their senses to find food.

They listen for prey with their two ears. Sharks have super hearing but not supersize ears. Their ears are hard to see. Each one is inside a tiny hole located behind the eye.

ear

gill slits

Breathing

Sharks breathe with their gills.
Water flows into their mouth.
Then, it goes over their gills
and out their gill slits.

Great whites use their sense
of smell the most.

Unlike people, sharks do not
sniff to catch a scent. The water
carries smells. It washes over
the shark's nose. The shark
follows the scents that might
lead to food.

Great whites also stick their nose out of the water. They can smell scents carried by the wind.

nostrils

Great whites can see very well in dark water. They have special cells in the back of their eyes. The cells work like mirrors. The light bounces off the back of their eyes. That makes it easier for sharks to see in the dark.

When great whites are trying to catch a meal, they roll their eyes back into their head. This helps protect the sharks' eyes from prey that is trying to escape.

Sharks have two senses that people do not have.
They use these senses to find food.

sensory pits

Special lines run down the side of a great white's body. The shark can feel when something is swimming nearby.

Small pits around the shark's face and head help find nearby prey, even if the shark cannot see it.

On the Hunt

Sharks use their speed, size, color, senses, and teeth to catch and eat food.

A great white watches a seal swimming overhead. The shark swims just deep enough to stay hidden. It also swims close enough to reach its prey before it escapes.

The shark waits and watches. Then, it swims upward with so much power it leaps out of the water.

Speedy Seals

Seals can turn as fast as a great white.

Stalking and hiding doesn't always work. The prey is often quick and gets away.

Big seals bite and scratch and can injure the shark.

Seafood Dinner

Great whites only eat meat. Younger sharks eat smaller prey. Bigger sharks eat bigger prey.

blue groupers

harbor seals

California sea lions

cape fur seals

elephant seals

jumbo squid

sea turtles

Powerful Predators

When people hear the word "shark," the big jaws and sharp teeth of a great white might come to mind. Great whites are not the biggest or the smallest sharks. But they might be the most famous!

Great whites' strength, size, and hunting skills make them powerful predators.

A Predator Becomes Prey

Great whites have only two predators: orcas and humans.

These same things can also make people fear them. But people are a bigger danger to sharks than sharks are to people. Threats like pollution and getting caught in fishing nets can hurt these animals.

Great whites can be fierce and fragile all at once.

Glossary

Gills
the body parts that sharks use to breathe

Predator
an animal that hunts and eats other animals

Prey
an animal hunted by a predator

Pup
a baby shark

Seal
a mammal that lives in the sea

Orca
a toothed mammal also called a killer whale

Index

Quiz

Answer the questions to see what you have learned. Check your answers in the key below.

1. True or False: A shark can fold its fins.

2. What is a shark's skeleton made of?

3. Why do great whites stick their nose out of the water?

4. What happens when a shark loses a tooth?

5. How do sharks breathe?

1. False 2. The same material as a person's ears 3. To smell
4. A tooth from the row behind replaces it 5. With their gills